ONE
FLESH

POEMS

ONE
FLESH

POEMS

OBED LADINY

Published November 18, 2018

ISBN 978-0-578-40264-2 pbk

Life is a flower of which love is the honey.

—Victor Hugo

Contents

Author's Note

These poems were written with various anonymous-person perspectives in mind. A window from each of their lives is slightly cracked open for the reader to eavesdrop on their movements and words through an accessible free-verse poetic style.

We all know of marriages and relationships in general that begin beautifully and end happily ever after, but this book doesn't paint such picture-perfection throughout its poems. A real-life relationship between a man and a woman—aside from Facebook and other social-media photos of bliss—actually does not follow a seamless line of untainted existence for most of us, whether we are religious, agnostic, atheistic, or simply secular in our world view. The human flesh is the common denominator connecting us all in this journey as imperfect beings striving for unity, completeness, and perfection in relation to one another.

This isn't a how-to-book, or even one with the intention of swaying the reader to one direction or a particular view. It is one that reveals a picture here and another there that the reader might relate to. Therefore, it can serve as a cathartic experience in realizing we are not alone in whatever happens to us in the process of building relationships.

The poems were not compiled for the purpose of answering questions concerning love and marriage. In that respect, it will surely come short for some readers. Rather, it presents lives and images that simply remind the reader of circumstances in or around his or her own life. What one reader takes from a poem may not be the same for another; that's part of the freedom of interpretation and beauty of poetry.

I

Marriage is a three-ring circus:
engagement ring, wedding ring, and suffering.

—*Unknown Source*

No More Favors

Do me no favors
if your motives fall right back to your hand.

Do me no favors
if not in the spirit of St. Teresa.

Do me no favors
if I've become a child beneath your shadow.

Do me no favors
if you must speak with silence and parables.

Do me no favors
if 111 and puck lips display on your face.

Do me no favors
if you'll broadcast your rolling list of good deeds.

Do me no favors
if they're done with bloody knives behind my back.

Do me no favors
if this means I must sell you my soul.

I'd rather walk without warmth, sleep out
like an alley cat, carry pangs of hunger,

die in the streets
than have you do me any more favors.

Recurring Talk

I'll sleep tonight,
though I toss
and turn
in the dark,
trapped
within our conversation film
of hours ago.
Daylight

will come
with all
its regular
demands,
and ain't nobody

got time
to wait
for a heart
to patch itself
back out
on the stage of day.

One Flesh

pebbles scratch,
deposit sand
on their hearts

gold ring burns
fourth finger
to an unbearable itch

~ ~ ~

hornets fly out of their mouths,
spread to corridors
into their children's ears

once they leaped
eager as deer
into this jagged sawteeth

What I'm Worth

If you don't think so,
perhaps I should start celebrating
me.

Let the champagne burst
in all directions; buy a cupcake
with sprinkled, whipped
cream, a candle on top
saluting tragedy.

Am I weighed down?
A little selfishness
brings back life.

I'll chase no more—
your turn.

What Some Third Parties Always Wanted to Say Out Loud but Never Dared

I won't be a judge
in your domestic disputes.
Each storyteller has a hook.
No one wants correction.
I'll excuse myself.
You may knock each other's
teeth out, make the other's
eyes swollen over nonsense.
You'll exchange threats and dares.
I'll go back into my own world.
Leave me to my cocoon where
you can almost hear a pin drop.
Life has more pressing matters
to be concerned and unbending about.
Many are screwed-up
with their sanity hanging by a thread.
I wake up early, off to work,
return home, enjoy evenings, and go
to bed. To Caesar what is Caesar's.
To God what is God's. Peace
with everyone as much as possible.
Maybe I'm getting old.

My energy for stupidity
is decreasing. Our problems
are life's challenges;
they have us by the throat, then
walk pass our graves.

The Children

are their cute oblivious
saviors, strong ropes
tied around a tree stump
with other ends
gleefully dangling from a cliff.

The Family

                           is a puzzle,

each piece interconnected

                           making a whole,

a system,

                           an ever growing entity,

a government

                           producing

extended governments.

                           heavens,

or hells

under roofs

                           extending

with multiplication

                           into a society

spreading out

                           into governments,

into the world

                where   somebody—continents
away,

has something of your face…

                and it all started with a stare

                and a smile, an exchange of

cautious words, a hug, a kiss,

                an apple eaten together

                under that tree. A serpent smiles

at our future.

How Much

How much do I love you,
can be answered by
how much of a pull
in the tug of war
of words and reason—

how much of a beating
of words against the fortress
of your fortified mind—

how much of a pass
for the sake of sunny weather
and peaceful breeze—

how much of a risk,
having laid all the cards
down from my hands
where you can see them—

how much of a trust
to become a sorry mule
with a heart bruised
and still beats with fever?

A Walk with Reality

He walks the busy city street
with a briefcase in his right hand,
dark grey suit, and eyeglasses.

Sirens and shouting
one block away.
He will not turn back

home; there in the living room
stands his wife with bright
eyes and a smile. The children

hang on to the back of his neck
like cubs over a lion
on the carpet. He crosses

a crowded street with his loose
crooked tie and unbuttoned white collar—
an appearance he was taught to avoid.

Recess

Another train passes through their living room.
A lofty plant of large green leaves shake.

Her voice cracks. The infant
cries from the bedroom. Sentences

like thunderclaps rescind into trickles till nothing.

~ ~ ~

He cradles the child in his arms,
turns toward the window.

She returns to the living room,
reclines on the sofa,

stares at their picture on the wall.

Enmity

Kill the creature

    that infests your chest,

        it venoms your veins,

poisonous messenger

    possesses and deforms,

        drains joy,

creeps from beneath,

    flames dart wounds,

        hearts turn to stone.

Sucks your blood,

    records every wrong,

        a disease that cripples—

chews its vessel
to the end.

When Morning Comes

They blend well
with the silence of night.

Maybe one day
morning
will come,
finds their hearts
in pieces
scattered—
one to east,
the other
west.

The heart's
pulse
is willing,
contends
for the prize endings
of fairy tales
and Harlequins
at the end
of these
miles,
and it
will.
Defeat—
a kryptonite,

villain
and roommate,
moved in
the head
with luggage where
their victory
dwells,
refusing
to leave.

A Piercing

Wonder where your heart is?
The hints are weighty enough
for a poor pierced chest to explore,
in this, much ignorance is grace.

Senryu

a pretzel,
already baked, wish
disentanglement.

What If?

What if
there's still time
and prayers
aren't wasted words
sent to the wind
but strong hands
grabbing destiny
by the throat?

What if
the end
of their heart string
melody of years
is just a cruel joke
played by one
against the other,
where laughter rises
after a crippling sting?
What if... if what?

Dr. Jekyll & Mr. Hyde
Complex in Human Nature

They both walked into a captivating family home
painted white on the outside.
Their reflections were even on its golden gates. From
the outside, it appeared as other
dream homes around it. They predicted three floors:
two or three bedrooms,
     living room, kitchen,
          and possibly a basement.

Upon entering and
observing, they discovered it
had more rooms than the White House—
public rooms
     and inner rooms
          within each room;

closets,
     inner closets
          within each closet;

basement
     and other grounds
     under the basement,
          further grounds
          under those.

It had more grounds

than
   s
      u
         b
            ways
            or ancient

   c
      a
         t
            a
               combs.

They walked
   stumb
      ling
         with
            diz
               zi
                  ness

wondering
   how much
      lower
         can these

grounds
be.

Will they ever make it back
to the living room,
the front door,
the sidewalk,
the streets under the clouds and
sun, to their world of fireworks?

Who would ever believe them if they should tell?
Who would ever understand?
Who would ever?

The Pendulum of
Human Love

Where do you sit or stand
when your world swings like a rocking chair
or a pendulum behind an hourglass?
You can go on eating meat
or live only on water and vegetables.
You can join lion-like soldiers
or monks in monastery basements.
You can brush humiliation sands off your shoulders
or help with the burying.

You're not a detached spirit,
but who says life must go on?
The bar of your worth has reached a low,
and you wonder whether to laugh hysterically
or fill your cup with rain.
Now you know why
many have taken the forbidden
coward's exit.
Are you struck?
Still trust in mortals?

The heart of the purest Man on Earth
did break and spill, bled in good faith
for an investment.
And you—
who the hell are you?

II

The difficulty with marriage is that we fall in love
with a personality, but must live with a character.

—Peter de Vries (1910-1993),
American editor and novelist

When His Teenage World Scratched the World of Profoundness

He heard a knock on the door, looked out
through the living room window.
She stood there waiting—a neighbor
who lived three houses from him.

Her woolly braids extended down her shoulders.
Her oval face and thick red lips
harmonized with her caramel skin.
In her hand, the letter
was folded in half.

He slowly released the curtain,
walking backwards.

Another knock on the door...
And another.

His brothers, in silence, knew
from what they saw in his face.

Back to the window,
he watched her walk away
with a purse on one shoulder, and then
he realized—the profoundness
of this other world.

Journeys to the
American Dream

Dive your nose in black coffee at Joe's Café,
    awake, awake,
        the girls need Mattel dolls and a playhouse
    tomorrow.

What if you return home one day, only to tell them
    you were sent off with a pink slip in hand,
    and have to watch their wondering eyes stare?

Dive your head in the men's restroom sink,
    awake, awake,
        the boys need toy soldiers and mini-Corvettes
    tomorrow.

What if you tell yourself, 'Hell
    to the American dream',
    snore under your cozy blanket till sundown?

Honey moves around in the kitchen
    in her pink Victoria's Secret lingerie,
    strangely silent,
    cracks your eggs in a white ceramic bowl.

Dive your head in a warm shower,
    awake, awake,
    you'll want her signature eggs rising up
    tomorrow.

She Still Manages

to put a Mount Everest
plate of spaghetti
on his reading table.

He told himself he'd eat out.
She was supposed to remain
deaf, dumb, and allergic
to his presence.

Here he is saying *thank you*
for the dinner she brought
fresh from the kitchen.

He'll wait till she leaves,
and reminds himself
to masticate it
slowly with disinterest.

An Acquaintance
Contemplates Forty

Near 40, he questions
what time is there
to retrieve the lost years
in his marriage,
fatherhood,
re-candle Romeo & Juliet,
and academia
anyhow?

Maybe there's space
for dreaming
or maybe he'll soon meet
that concrete wall.

Is it still about them?
What about the children?
Plenty he'd like to say.
Mountains he wishes to climb.

Many of his comrades
have lists of accomplishments;
he has a list
of dreams.

How could he go on
looking at his face in the mirror
each day
without the list?

He Has Dreams

He has dreams—he's that somebody
with his head held high in this society,
though it races towards a dead end.

He has dreams—their children will focus,
make something of themselves with the tools
of progress in their hands.

He has dreams—he sees her in the future,
walking and strutting like a queen;
he wants her in new dresses.

He has dreams—she stands at a distance,
he says come, she runs toward him and jumps.
He catches her in his arms like they're newlyweds.

He has dreams—of joined lips, of hearts
echoing across each other, their streams blending.
Yes, he has dreams

of them and the children looking up at Orion's star,
smiling, and arriving at home…
arriving… at home.

Solitude

Displacement
calls me back
into your arms.
Hostile cold world
draws me into you.

I hike toward your cave;
there, find a haven,
light your recesses
with my lamp, warm
myself within your cloak.

After-School Subway Teens

He's the king
of the world.
Pretty boy
with earrings
and backward cap.
She's the queen
on his lap. She
chews and pops
her bubblegum
then flaunts her
crow hair in his face.

She's probably some man's
daughter, who waits
for her safe retreat
at home. And the boy
could be some woman's
son, who waits for him
to enter the house
and rush pass her
with his headphones
deafening as he
enters his room.

Her giggles. His
octopus arms;
she peels them back
one by one, not fast
and stern enough
as she ought.

When Her Wine Runs Out

No exit doors,
but she'll defy expectations
like the brave ones
who developed wings
they never had

and flew out windows,
against the rules, gone
looking for life
again.

Your Independence Day Meal

you lay, eyes closed,
feline whiskers
near plate of food
half-eaten on grass,
under a tree shade
in front of the building.
conflagrations must've
kept you up all night
staring into dark skies
exploding, but somebody
graced you this humid day
and made up for disturbing
your peace. i ain't mad
to see you fat. better you
find a warm heart
in these hard times
than to have nobody
in this world.

III

To be fully seen by somebody, then, and be loved anyhow—this is a human offering that can border on miraculous.

—Elizabeth Gilbert, Committed:
A Skeptic Makes Peace with Marriage

Trampling

What's wrong with you?
Stand up for yourself.

Your honor rolls in the dust.
Her stories advertise your faults.
You never say stop.
I wish you would.

You sit there, take it all in—
 a big useless lion,
no retort of some kind,
or show of manly pride.
Speak and shut her up,
but a mysterious strength
holds your tongue.

~ ~ ~

I'm in my bed of flowers,
and have a home to keep.
I recall your silence.

You took it like a man—
intelligent, committed.
By your silence,
you must've agreed with God
to let *Him* do your talking.

I've got to take with me—

your silence under the trampling.
Mistook it for weakness.

If only it would come with ease.
There are times I don't wanna be a fool.
I need the strength to appear weak.

Your blood should have curled.
I waited to see you burst
like a thermometer.

Two Fools

They were two fools willing to take a chance
and bet on each other against the whole wide
world; hungry fools with hot peppered lips,

and the sun burning in their bosoms.
They were like sheep carried to the slau-altar
by their own willing anticipation.

Life beat them awake with its belt, and chained
their feet to its stalls, so that neither of them
could run. They watched each other

over the years die and reborn,
                die and reborn,
                die and reborn. Their skins

peeled against rugged earth. They're weary
and worn, but proud with mixed feelings
for the chains—their altruistic act.

Roads

Wonder where this is going.
Reminds me of Frost's poem, *The Road
Not Taken*. It's like missing an exit
in an unfamiliar highway
or mistakenly coming out of one
where we should have kept on going,
and if we're lucky
we'd reach our destinations
still in our right minds—weary,

but freshly scented
as if we haven't been scorched by summers
and frozen by winters—
all at once,

so when old acquaintances see us
they'd say 'Gosh, ya'll haven't changed one bit',
and we'd believe 'em.

What He and She Said

She says, *This train isn't going anywhere.*
He says, I*t is, and it will. You'll see.*
She says, *I'm getting off.*
He says, *Some minor difficulties. That's all.*
She looks away, *The hour is late.*
He stares at his shoes, *Regretfully so, but we'll get there.*
She scratches the edge of her nails, *Another train
will be quick and comfortable.*
He looks at his watch, *The Conductor
admonished riders' patience.*
She stands up, *I'm getting off and waiting for the next.*
He sighs, *See you at desired station.*
She stands one foot out, looks far
into the distance, then at him.

Down on Dusts

On folded knees, raised hands, tears
circulate in the heart's river.
rising incense, sweet savor,
sky staring—a genuine friend.

Unwanted

Look how the sun shines
this morning.
Hasn't blazed like that
in a long time.
You wake up
without a care in the world.
You place your barefeet
off the bed
and unto the cold floor,
and the feeling
is like no other from the past.
Outside your window
the world is waiting for you,
and you're energized
more than ever, to step out and say hello
fiercely, with a confidence
long held back and imprisoned
until now—sprinkled
with anger and peace.
When you think about the years
gone by,
you slump almost depressed
out of your mind
only to escape into the present where
you hear your own voice say
'I made it past the flames'

and you deserve
to love yourself. Your problem
was you thought
it was wrong to high-five yourself.
You thought you'd go to hell
for giving yourself a hug.
You thought if you just loved genuinely
and blindly then you'd be loved
cuddled like a newborn
entering the world in return. The world
taught you how foolish
you were and your aching chest
taught you how immature
you were and how
dangerously you stood trusting
the edge of mountains
like a child. You were impressed
with them
and never saw what you saw
to really be plains
you carved into mountains.
Funny how a simple '*I do*'
has brought you to the edge
of existence
only to laugh at you
loudly and say
you 'big dumb fool',
who lied to you that this side of the world
is heaven, when we all know

that we're inmates
guilty for having been too shallow
and inexperienced fish
caught in its hooks, but now
toughened up with hearts
made solid by the hand of trials.
Surprised, are you?
Where did you come from then?

At Last, A Home of Our Own

First tour through this house,
almost any guest would gasp
at its many elegant rooms,
front lawn, and spacious backyard.

Its rooms were empty
for some months
before we could fill its cabinets and closets,
and purchase furniture.
Even now the central heating system
needs fixing as the cold season draws near.
A neighbor said the costs to replace the old one
would be in the thousands,
and we don't have that kind of money.
We'll have to wait.

Wait like we always do.
We've experienced disappointments before,
and seasons of coldness
have never failed us.

We know how to smile
like the way this house opens itself
to the envy of family, friends, and strangers.
We know how to smile in want.

Step by step, year
after year no matter how long it takes,
we'll better our home.

Still the One

Walk with me near the river;
we'll listen to the robins sing
in the trees. Take my hand.
We'll show them
how dramatists work with lights.

Come to the water bank with me;
let's go fishing down there
and talk about what we know. Look!
Two Camellias
in their shrub are swaying
side to side in the soft wind.

What appears, must be.
What isn't, ought to be.
What was, can be. Sing
this Shania Twain song with me.

Enduring Roses

These roses are dying in the crystal vase
with their stems in the water still.
They're shriveling maybe out of hunger,
maybe out of no sunshine; or,
maybe it's about time they die.
Nothing lives forever.

Yes, they were beautiful, possibly three days ago.
They meant something then, symbolic of life.
Now, they're corpses, dry and crisp—
ready for the bin. Everything dies.

Lovers and their budding hearts of romance,
deplete their life's savings on wedding dresses,
tuxes, limos, reception halls, invitations, dozens of
photos for albums of happy memories, only—
to die like flowers later. They sometimes die sooner
than these roses hanging from this crystal vase.

But I've heard of enemies putting down their arms
and countries settling disputes.
I've heard of forgotten wedding albums
found in deep hidden places of the earth.
I've seen, after a season of winter,
newly sprouted leaves.
I've heard of dying plants coming back to life.

I've heard of admirable, stubbornly breathing,
wounded, but surviving couples—
that just wouldn't shrivel up and die.
I've heard of enduring roses.

Epilogue:
Well-Known People Giving
Their Two Cents' Worth

Here are some quotes from well-known people, both ancient and postmodern, bearing light on this topic:

In all the world, there is no heart for me like yours. In all the world, there is no love for you like mine.

– Maya Angelou

Lots of people want to ride with you in the limo, but what you want is someone who will take the bus with you when the limo breaks down.

– Oprah Winfrey

I have decided to stick with love. Hate is too great a burden to bear.

– Martin Luther King, Jr.

Love is of all passions the strongest, for it attacks simultaneously the head, the heart and the senses.

– Lao Tzu

Love is a smoke made with the fume of sighs.

– William Shakespeare

The opposite of love is not hate; it's indifference.

– Elie Wiesel

Love is composed of a single soul inhabiting two bodies.

– Aristotle

There is no remedy for love but to love more.

– Henry David Thoreau

If there is such a thing as a good marriage, it is because it resembles friendship rather than love.

– Michel de Montaigne (1533 – 1592),
French philosopher and essayist

Keep your eyes wide open before marriage, and half-shut afterwards.

– Benjamin Franklin (1706 – 1790),
American statesman, scientist and philosopher

After marriage, a woman's sight becomes so keen that she can see right through her husband without looking at him, and a man's so dull that he can look right through his wife without seeing her.

– Helen Rowland (1875 – 1950),
American journalist and humorist

The difficulty with marriage is that we fall in love with a personality, but must live with a character.

– Peter de Vries (1910 – 1993),
American editor and novelist

A happy marriage is a long conversation which always seems too short.

– Andre Maurois (1885 – 1967),
French writer

In marriage do thou be wise; prefer the person before money; virtue before beauty; the mind before the body.

– William Penn (1644 – 1718),
British religious leader

Three things drive a man outdoors; smoke, a leaking roof and a scolding wife.

– Proverb

When two people are under the influence of the most violent, most insane, most delusive, and most transient passions, they are required to swear that they will remain in that excited, abnormal, and exhausting condition continuously until death do them part.

– George Bernard Shaw (1856 – 1950),
Irish writer

If it weren't for marriage, men and women would have to fight with total strangers.

– Unknown Source

Marriage is a three-ring circus: engagement ring, wedding ring, and suffering.

– Unknown Source

To catch a husband is an art; to hold him is a job.
> – Simone de Beauvoir (1908 – 1986),
> French novelist and essayist

The most happy marriage I can imagine to myself would be the union of a deaf man to a blind woman.
> – Samuel Taylor Coleridge (1799 – 1850),
> British poet, critic, and philosopher

Both marriage and death ought to be welcome: The one promises happiness, doubtless the other assures it.
> – Mark Twain (1835 – 1910),
> American humorist, writer, and lecturer

I first learned the concepts of non-violence in my marriage.
> – Mahatma Gandhi (1868 – 1948),
> Preeminent leader of Indian nationalism

To be fully seen by somebody, then, and be loved anyhow—this is a human offering that can border on miraculous.
> – Elizabeth Gilbert,
> *Committed: A Skeptic Makes Peace with Marriage*

To the Reader

It means a lot to me that you purchased One Flesh - Poems. You could have picked any other book to read, but you chose this one. I am grateful!

If you enjoyed this poetry book and found some benefit in reading it, I'd like to hear from you and hope that you could take some time to post a review on the platform you purchased it or whichever platform you prefer to inform others of your discovery. Thank you.

About the Author

OBED LADINY is an educator and a frequent participant in literature and poetry forums. He enjoys writing contemporary free-verse poems that deal with society, relationships, places, history, religion, and opinionated epiphanies from reflections on various topics. Some of his poems first appeared in *TWJ Magazine, the Poems-For-All Project, In Between Hangovers, Red Fez, and Torrid Literature Journal.* Ladiny is a native of Haiti, raised in Ft. Lauderdale, Florida and later became a resident of New York.

My Thoughts for Today

My Thoughts for Today

My Thoughts for Today

My Thoughts for Today

_____

_____

_____

_____

_____

_____

_____

_____

_____

_____

_____

_____

_____

_____

_____

_____

_____

_____

_____

_____

My Thoughts for Today

My Thoughts for Today

My Thoughts for Today

My Thoughts for Today

My Thoughts for Today

My Thoughts for Today

My Thoughts for Today

My Thoughts for Today

My Thoughts for Today

My Thoughts for Today

My Thoughts for Today

My Thoughts for Today

_____

_____

_____

_____

_____

_____

_____

_____

_____

_____

_____

_____

_____

_____

_____

_____

_____

_____

_____

_____

My Thoughts for Today

My Thoughts for Today

_____

_____

_____

_____

_____

_____

_____

_____

_____

_____

_____

_____

_____

_____

_____

_____

_____

_____

_____

_____

My Thoughts for Today

My Thoughts for Today

My Thoughts for Today

My Thoughts for Today

My Thoughts for Today

My Thoughts for Today

_____

_____

_____

_____

_____

_____

_____

_____

_____

_____

_____

_____

_____

_____

_____

_____

_____

_____

_____

_____

_____

My Thoughts for Today

My Thoughts for Today

My Thoughts for Today

_____

_____

_____

_____

_____

_____

_____

_____

_____

_____

_____

_____

_____

_____

_____

_____

_____

_____

_____

My Thoughts for Today

Also by Obed Ladiny

Cracked Flutes: Blues from the Soul - Poems, Volume 1
Cracked Flutes: Blues from the Soul - Poems, Volume 2

Made in the USA
Monee, IL
30 March 2023